Hi, I'm Jason.

When I was a kid I got lost at the seaside.

It was really scary.

This is what happened.

Mum and Steve took me to the seaside for the day.
We went to the beach.
It was ace. There was so much to see.
Steve and I saw this brilliant speedboat.

Different landscapes

After lunch, Mum and Steve fell asleep.
I went over to some older lads.
They were playing football.
They let me play too.
I got really hot.
I really fancied an ice cream, so I went to get one.
I didn't tell Mum or Steve I was going.
They were still asleep.

Saying where you are going

I bought an ice cream and I went back to the beach.
But it all looked different.
I couldn't see Mum or Steve…or the speedboat!
I couldn't see the older lads playing football.
I didn't know where I was!

Looking for landmarks

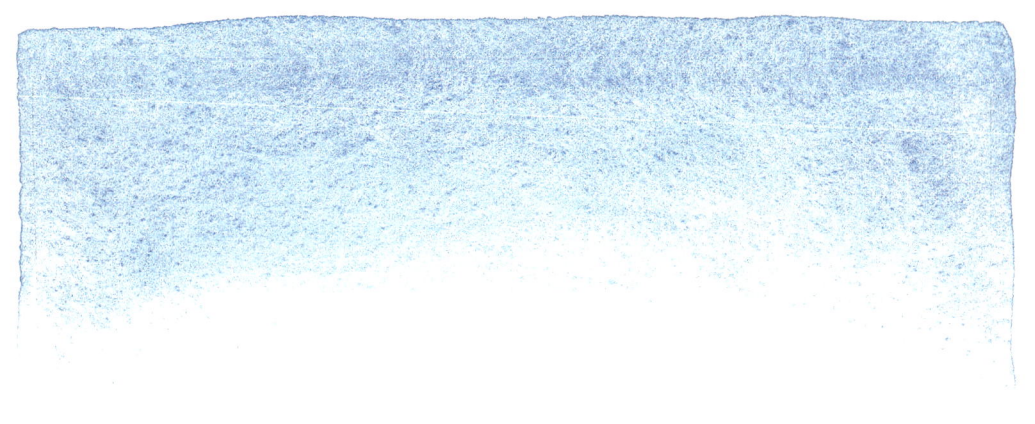

I felt sick with worry.

Where were they?

How was I going to find them again?

I told myself I had to stay calm.

Importance of staying calm

I ran along the beach.

A man asked me if I was OK.

He said he'd help me, but he looked a bit dodgy!

I didn't know who he was, so I just ran off.

Strangers who offer to help

It was getting dark.
I went up to the road.
I looked for someone to help me,
like a policeman.
Then a woman walked by with her baby.
So I asked her for help.

Who to ask for help

"Let's find a nice safe place to sit down," she said.

We waited by the ice cream van.

"Let's wait here for a few minutes," she said.

"If they don't come soon, I'll ring for help."

Then I saw Mum and Steve.
Was I glad to see them!

Doing the sensible thing

Learning from experience

Now, when I am in a new place I look for landmarks, I work out where I am. I always tell someone where I am going, and I keep my mobile phone with me, just in case!